Someone Has Died

A Children's Guide to Surviving a Loved One's Death

by Tracy Renee Lee, FDIC QCFH

Illustrated by Matthew McGown

Tracy Renee Lee

Copyright © 2014 Tracy Renee Lee

All rights reserved.

ISBN – 10 0989444724
ISBN – 13 9780989444729

Tracy Renee Lee

Note to Mom & Dad

Dear Mom & Dad,

This book was written with your little ones in mind. Death can be a difficult thing to endure as an adult, and children are equally affected at the loss of a loved one.

As you read this book with your little ones, be mindful of their comments and observations. Encourage them to discuss the concepts within these pages.

I have included photographs of Butter and Lady so that your children can see they are real animals. This story is true and Butter and Lady live at the funeral home with me and my family.

For the first few days, before the funeral of your loved one, please read and reread this book, out loud with your children.

Someone Has Died helps you discuss the concepts of loss and memorialization with your children. This discussion will better prepare them for what they will experience before, during and after, the memorialization services. It will also help you broach a subject that can be difficult to address, especially when you are grieving.

I have designed this book to be purse and diaper bag compatible for mom, and breast pocket or back pocket compatible for dad. The book is bendable, so fold it in half if need be. Please take it with you to the various services and events of funeral week. Allow your children to have it with them at all times. Their new friends, Butter and Lady will help your little ones feel free to discuss their feelings and perceptions with you, and remember the importance of "Minding Their Manners" during this stressful time.

Tracy Renee Lee

DEDICATION

This book is dedicated to my darling girls.
Without them, life would not be worth living.
Oh, and their two dogs,
Lady, so strong, yet gentle with those she loves;
and Butter, a mountain of energy who loves everyone she meets.

"Lady" "Butter"
"Best Friends Forever"

0

Someone has Died

ACKNOWLEDGMENTS

Matthew McGown

A talented artist I met attending a funeral at my funeral home.
Thank you Matthew for working with me on this project.
I appreciate your professionalism, flexibility and time management skills.
Also, I love your art.

Tracy Renee Lee

Someone has Died

SURVIVING A LOVED ONE'S DEATH

Tracy Renee Lee

This is Butter.

Butter is a poodle.

Butter is the sweetest puppy ever.

She has a special job.

She is a grief therapy dog.

People are sad when someone has died.

Butter works at the funeral home helping people to not be so sad.

Family and friends come to the funeral home to have a funeral when someone has died.

A funeral is a ceremony where family and friends gather to remember their loved one.

When sad families come to the funeral home,

Butter comes out to cuddle them

and help them feel

a little better.

Sometimes she gives them a big hug,

and sometimes she gives them kisses.

When someone has died, people are very sad.

They are sad because they loved the person who died very much.

They are sad because they will not be able to

see or do things with this person anymore.

Butter's special friend is Lady.

Lady is a miniature schnauzer.

Butter and Lady play together every day.

Butter would be very sad if anything happened to Lady.

When someone has died, they are no longer here with us.

We can only remember them

and think of the fun things we did with them.

We cannot see or talk to them because they have died.

They have gone away.

Butter knows when someone has died,

their friends and family

will never see them again.

She tries to play with

their friends and

give them love.

Butter knows even though their

special friend has died, they still need other friends.

When someone has died, they are buried in the earth or sea.

If they want to be cremated,

their ashes may be buried or scattered at a place that is special; perhaps the sea.

They usually decide what to do with their body before they die.

They tell someone they love and trust what they would like to have done with their body, once they die.

Butter likes to bury her chew toys out by an old pecan tree.

When she gets a new chew toy,

she runs out to the tree and sits there

while she chews her new toy.

She likes to do this because

it is peaceful by the old pecan

tree and she can remember

all of her old chew toys.

If you know someone who is dying, it is a good idea to let them know that you love them.

You could make them a card and take it to their house or the hospital.

A sweet card helps people feel happier when they are sick.

A nice drawing or a picture of you would probably help them feel happier too.

If your friend is too sick for visitors, you could send your card or gift by mail.

Butter and Lady love to get things in the mail.

They go out to the mailbox every day

because Susan (their mail carrier)

always has a tasty bone for them.

They love tasty bones.

Some people think when you die, your new home is heaven.

They think you go there, and you live with Jesus.

Some people think you live with Buddha.

Where do you think people live once they die?

Butter thinks when someone has died they go to heaven

and see all of their old friends.

Maybe she is right.

ABOUT THE AUTHOR

Tracy Renee Lee began her professional career as a licensed day care owner and provider for fifteen years before becoming a funeral director. Her love of children has motivated her to write a series of books addressing grief for the very young.

Tracy is a funeral director, author and professional speaker. She writes books and weekly bereavement articles related to understanding and coping with grief. She delivers powerful messages and motivates audiences in "Grief Recovery".

It is her life's mission to comfort the bereaved and help them live on.

www.ingramcontent.com/pod-product-compliance
Lightning Source LLC
LaVergne TN
LVHW071031070426
835507LV00002B/108